EAT TO RUN

Holistic nutrition for the ultra-marathon runner

Stutisheel Lebedev

Eat to Run
Holistic nutrition for the ultra-marathon runner
Stutisheel Oleg Lebedev

Stutisheel Oleg Lebedev is the first runner from the Post-Soviet Countries to finish the world longest certified race, the Sri Chinmoy Self-Transcendence 3100-mile race. He ran the 3100-mile race for the first time in 2004, and ran it ten more times afterwards. In 2014 he achieved his best finish time: 48 days 3 hours 57 minutes and 19 seconds (an average of 103.6 km/day). For more than 21 years he has been practicing meditation on the path of spiritual Master Sri Chinmoy.

This book contains his firsthand experience of holistic nutrition, at the world longest multi-day race. It is aimed at everyone who seeks to lead a harmonious life and to unfold his/her ultimate potential.

Editor: Bhadra Kleinman
Photo credits: Alakananda, Jowan, Arpan, Prabhakar.

Additional information
www.Stutisheel.org
www.3100.Lebedev.org.ua

All rights reserved. No part of this book may be reproduced in any form without the written permission of the author: stutisheel@gmail.com

ISBN-13: 978-1505213553
ISBN-10: 150521355X

© 2016 Oleg Lebedev

Reader's comments

Never have I seen any truths on nutrition so well-tested as those you find in EAT TO RUN! While most nutritionists write about what they have read in others' books, exceptionally good nutritionists test their findings in their own lives. But in *this* book, you find nutritional evidence tested under the hardest pressures one could possibly imagine. Every word was checked repeatedly in the world's hardest crash test for the holistically fittest runners ever. This race was designed by the creator of a self-transcendence-experience for spiritual growth going far beyond normal human physical limitations. To learn of any result of such an impossibility-traveler is a boon we normal mortals usually cannot receive. To implement these self-givingly offered results in our own lives of inner and outer running is to equip our frail bodies with invincible strength. Just do it!

Abarita Danzer, *Swiss food manufacturer, author of several books on food and sports, and marathon runner with a Personal Best of 2:31, at age 41. www.Soyana.ch*

To run the 3100-mile race is a monumental achievement. To finish it seven times is an experience beyond the mind's ability to comprehend. In this book, Stutisheel offers some ideas that will help anyone contemplating running multi-day races build a nutritional framework upon which to base their experiments

Abichal Watkins, *3100 mile runner, editor of the www.Multidays.com*

I like it!

Dr. Kausal C. Cortella *Ph.D. Vedic Psychology, N.D., Race Medical Staff; CEO of the Swiss Optimal Living Society, www.SOLSociety.ch*

Holistic nutrition for the ultra-marathon runner

Contents

Reader's comments•3

Contents•5

Today's Everyday Automobile•6

Introduction•8

I Eat No Being•12

Theory And Practice Of Holistic Nutrition•14

Kinesiological Muscle Testing•21

Alkaline Balance •25

Ionized Water•28

Fats And Their Breakdown•37

Vitamins And Supplements•39

The Secret Ingredient•44

Recommended Books For Further Reading•48

Today's Everyday Automobile

Today's car, with its improved performance and mileage, is no accident of engineering. It is based on the results of trials and testing. Certainly, much of that testing occurs in the labs of the car manufacturer, but a larger part comes from the real-life high-performance-testing of the racing circuit, where cars are pushed to their limits competitively. The high-performance engineering of Formula 1 and NASCAR circuits trickle down to the everyday performance of the cars you and I drive to and from work!

The Self-Transcendence 3100-Mile Race is the world's longest certified foot race. Yes, it is run by humans, not cars! And what makes it even more difficult is that it is not a point-to-point race where you can experience new terrain every day. It is run on a half-mile course on the sidewalks of Queens, New York, in the middle of the summer in New York City. It is, perhaps, one of the most grueling and challenging of human endeavors. I say this, not because

Holistic nutrition for the ultra-marathon runner

I was one of those runners (I wasn't), but simply because, objectively observed, the accomplishment is staggering. The runner has to average 60 miles a day (i.e., over two marathons a day) for the duration of the race—52 days. Average means there are days where the runner achieves less than 60 miles, which means that there have to be days where he runs more than 60 miles! And to succeed, everything has got to be in-tune: the body has to be strong and well-nourished, the emotions must be in check, the mind must be clear in intent, and the spiritual will must be one-pointed in purpose. Should any of these elements fail, the participant's performance will falter, or perhaps he/she will not succeed.

Stutisheel participated in 10 starts of the 3100-Mile Race and what he has discovered is that, like the Formula 1 circuit, the race serves as a testing ground for everyday life. In a very brief time, what works nutritionally, mentally and spiritually can be tested, and whether you're training for a race, or for simply optimizing your everyday life, these same lessons can make your life healthier and stronger, inwardly and outwardly. He is happy to share them with you.

Dr. Pradhan Balter, *Chiropractor to the 3100-Mile Race Runners, author of the book "A Twenty-First Century Seeker"*

Introduction

I would like to make it clear from the very beginning that I'm neither a medical doctor nor a theoretician. I'm a long-distance runner. Since 2004, I have finished the longest certified race in the world, the 3100-mile Self-Transcendence race, nine times. My best time is 48 days 3 hours 57 minutes and 19 seconds, which I achieved in 2014. I'm continuing to participate in the race.

Nutrition during a race is not the main thing to consider when we talk about distances under 42 km, except perhaps during the period of training and preparation. However, when we participate in races of 100 km, 12 hours, or 24 hours, let alone the 6- and 10-day races and 3100-mile race, we need a well-planned nutritional strategy. I must say that my participation in ultra-distance races has seriously influenced my daily diet as well. During the race and under severe loads, everything manifests faster than in our day-to-day life, including right and wrong decisions. But the experience you get from unfolding your capacities is universal.

In the book I will jump back and forth from the race diet to every day food habits, because in general I guess this should be the one culture, especially when we are talking about races with duration of 50+ days.

Holistic nutrition for the ultra-marathon runner

My finish in the 3100-Mile Race 2014

Modern medicine has yet to explore and unscramble this field of endurance. In my turn I can tell you which food products, supplements and vitamins work, and which don't. When I tried to find appropriate experts for my multi-day race preparation back in 2004 I turned to consulting physicians, team doctors and various multi-level representatives. However, the best they could offer was how to keep my peak performance for a 5-day period.

The thing is, I needed to keep going for 50 days!

Thus, we have what we have - about 34 runners who have been attempting and finishing the annual Sri Chinmoy Self-Transcendence 3100-Mile Race in New York City for 17 years now - is a group of people who know better than anyone else what their bodies and spirits need to endure such exertions.

Granted, during the race we are assisted by doctors who can find the 'bug' and suggest how to solve it. Chiropractors gave me a lot, too. Strictly speaking, my approach to nutrition and other aspects was formed slowly from my racing experience and doctors' tips and hints. But there were situations when doctors just shrugged their shoulders at the fact that, despite eating the same vitamins and supplements, I didn't have enough energy to run that day, while the next day I was almost flying without any changes in my diet. Not everything depends solely on diet. There is a hidden factor rooted in the very idea, the very sense and Vision of such amazing runs. I will try to lift the veil from the knowledge I gained from the races.

When I first started to deliver my workshops on the 3100-mile race, the answer to the popular questions on runners' diet has been that there was no secret in it and that it wasn't the main point. Now, after having finished seven races, I can assure you that proper diet is able to support, to unfold 100% of your potential given by Mother Nature, while the wrong diet can block your power and condemn you to unnecessary suffering and pain. Thus, it's quite important for the diet to be correct. When combined with the proper spiritual approach, preparation, attitude and motivation for such competitions, we can be surprised by our great abilities! By how our bodies are able to adjust to running 100 km each of the 50 days of a race, and then to recuperate completely after only 5 hours of sleep each night! Still, I don't consider myself special, and I believe that many people around me are capable of living far more active lives, and rising to loftier heights both in sports and life, than what they are doing currently. All the ingredients must come together: physical, financial, spiritual... However, there is one 'secret ingredient' that triggers the final result. I will talk about it in this book.

Everything I reveal here works 100% for me. Here is my timing for my eight finishes in the 3100-mile race:

    2004 - 53 days + 03:57:38
    2005 - 54 days + 07:15:40
    2006 - 54 days + 04:24:41
    2007 - 50 days + 12:21:25
    2008 - 50 days + 11:19:46
    2009 - 48 days + 12:42:46
    2011 - 52 days + 16:19:18
    2014 - 48 days + 03:57:19
    2015 - 50 days + 12:52:49

So, let's start the journey!

Stutisheel

I Eat No Being

The vast majority of ultra-marathon runners are vegetarians. Even those who had been meat eaters in the past eventually start to prefer a vegetarian diet. I've been following a vegetarian path for 21 years now - no meat, no fish. The race I'm talking about is the best touchstone for all the theories related here. Likewise, I can state with certainty that the statements about indispensable amino acids, deficiency of a vegetarian diet and things like that do not hold water. During these 21 years of life and participation in many extreme races, I have rebuilt my body several times, and I keep feeling better and better each day.

Google can help you find useful information on the composition of a vegetarian diet. Here I would like to mention the example of some famous vegetarians: Leonardo Da Vinci, Leo Tolstoy, Benjamin Franklin, Arthur Schopenhauer, Mahatma Gandhi, Albert Einstein, Carl Lewis and Muhammad Ali. I would like also to note that strict Ayurvedic practitioners refuse to treat meat-eaters. This is something to think about.

Trying to follow the most practical way of eating during the race, we always want to eat less, saving time, but still want to gain more energy. Animal food is not appropriate here, due to the great amount of energy expended for digestion, and the low efficiency output.

Holistic nutrition for the ultra-marathon runner

While the step toward vegetarianism is very important, it's only the beginning. It's not enough just to eliminate animal products from our diet. Everyone should eat a well-balanced diet; so much moreso athletes expending extraordinary amounts of energy.

At the time of my first race, I hardly knew what I should eat, knowing just a few things I had read in former participants' comments, and heard from several ultra-marathon runners I knew. It was surprising to me that all the doctors at the race recommended that I give up eating sweets, e.g., chocolate, sugary desserts, etc. I've learned that under constant repetitive activity, exertions like slow long-distance running, carbohydrates lose their leading status of 'fuel' because they are consumed too fast. Indeed, I've experienced a certain burst of energy after eating a candy, quickly followed by a slump when I felt even more exhausted than before.

This continued until I explored some statements like the following: fats make the main fuel for multi-day races, while proteins are responsible for building muscles. One of the pioneers of multi-day races, Trishul Cherns, told me about the zone diet: 40% carbohydrates, 30% proteins and 30% fats. The following menu can serve as an example: rice as the source of carbohydrates; soy cheese (tofu) for proteins accompanied by olive oil. Fats that work for me include olive oil, cashew, avocado, and ghee oils. Some of my co-runners consume milk, which I eliminated from my diet after food poisoning caused by milk and cheesecake. In addition to this, digestion of any milk becomes more difficult with age, let alone the quality of milk we buy in supermarkets nowadays...

Theory And Practice Of Holistic Nutrition

Speaking of a well-balanced diet, I must mention the holistic approach to the subject. The first time I heard about it was when my good friend, Abarita Danzer, the owner of the Swiss company "Soyana" which pioneered the development of a number of vegetarian food products, told me about the approach.

The main idea of holistic nutrition is to preserve the natural integrity of food components, and to avoid products which are not created by nature alone. A grain can be a good example of a natural food. Look at how balanced and complete it is, with its ability to sprout when planted in proper soil. It gives new life! How self-sufficient a grain is! Not only does it contain all the elements essential for a new plant, it has them also in a perfectly balanced form: bran layer, germ, cellulose, vitamins, minerals, proteins, and carbohydrates.

Nevertheless, food manufacturers have decided to improve on the things nature gave us. They have split the grain into different parts. The finest white flour contains only proteins and carbohydrates (starch). It is the part used most in our everyday diet. In coarse dark flour, some vitamins and minerals are present. The most precious, yet undervalued parts, the bran and germ are sold as animal fodder!

It's hard to imagine that white flour could ever give new life. Not only is it a product of a mechanical treatment, but also it is an artificial extract of elements that do not exist in pure form in nature. That means that this product may unbalance our system. And it does! During multi-day races, under great exertion, we reap what we have sown by our lifestyle, when our body just fails to perform normally. As you can see, our diet is just the tip of the iceberg. Granted, special diet right before a race is important, but what really matters is our everyday life and nutrition. I would like to mention that after my early races, I completely refused sugar and all food based on white flour. Imperfect health is too high a price for such food.

Honey and stevia are natural sweeteners that are acceptable if needed. By the way, though, most herbal teas taste more natural and have more depth without any sweetener at all.

Both during a race and in my everyday menu I prefer wholegrain cereals like unpolished rice, barley, oat, and my favorite - buckwheat.

Holistic approach will lead you in consuming not only natural products, but also help learning what is suitable specifically for you. We have biological legacy formed by our parents, our stomach is used to digest food that is growing in our region of living, we have biorhythms spreading along the day, we are under influence of sun which is greatly connected with our digestion... At first steps you need to understand, as your mission, your role in life is unique – so is your nutrition. Especially under extreme physical load. What is suitable for others may not help you. Therefore, you need to search for products, diet and regimen that will make specifically you stronger. You might be interested in visiting chiropractor and do kinesiological muscle testing to understand what is better for you. I will speak about that in the next chapter.

Both during a race and in my everyday menu I prefer wholegrain cereals like unpolished rice, barley, oat, and my favorite of course - buckwheat.

Holistic approach will lead you in consuming not only natural products, but also help learning what is suitable directly for you. We have biological legacy formed by our parents, our stomach is used to digest food that is growing in our region of living, we have biorhythms spreading along the day, we are under influence of sun which is greatly connected with our digestion… At first steps you need to understand, as your mission, your role in life is unique – so is your nutrition. Especially under extreme physical load. What is suitable for others may not help you. Therefore, you need to search for products, diet and regimen that will make directly you stronger. You might be interested in visiting chiropract and do kinesiological muscle testing to understand what is better for you. I will speak about that in the next chapter.

What I would really like to talk about is water. During my first races, I saw that many runners suffered from heartburn, especially in the afternoons. Tap water in New York is considered to be of drinking quality. However, under the loads we had, our bodies were more sensitive to everything, and that water turned out to be not so suitable

Holistic nutrition for the ultra-marathon runner

for us. All the meals and drinks cooked with it made our bodies rebel. The Slovakian runners started to buy bottled water, while I got a Brita water filter. Eventually the race cooks began to use purified water and sometimes even bought special structured Ojas waters from Switzerland. That brought great relief to us all. So, if you don't know what kind of water you might be provided with in strange places, I strongly advise you to take a portable water filter with you.

Intuitively, I know the benefit of an interval between a meal and a drink. Ancient practices of Ayurveda support this. It may not be that comfortable during the race, but still, it's possible to wait 10-20 minutes after a meal before you drink. During my everyday life I drink liquids 10-20 minutes before having a meal, and not less than half an hour afterwards. We will return to the subject of water again below, when I talk about antioxidants.

Regarding my dietary regime during the preparation period, I can say that I do not take food before my morning workout. It is believed that until 12 pm our bodies cleanse themselves of wastes and toxins, and that we must not strain it with intensive digestion before that time. Fruits, herbal tea or fresh juice can be perfect nutrition before 12 pm. Over the years I got used to such a regime, and now I don't feel hungry in the morning at all.

I'd like to add that I always take a bottle of water and some dried fruits and nuts (hazelnuts, dried apricots, raisins, prune, apples) for snacks during running workouts of over 1 and 1/2 hours. My final preparation includes a few workouts of over 60 km, taking about 7 hours in total – under these circumstances it is essential to eat during the workout. As a rule, I choose a 5 km lap for my workout, and put all my snacks under some tree, and have something each time I go past it.

During the 3100-mile race, which starts at 6 in the morning every day, I tend to wake up my digestion really gently by having a teaspoon of Chavanprash, then yogurt, bananas and other fruits. After several laps (1 lap= 883 m) I sense when my body has awakened enough for other foods. (I don't wait till 12 pm to eat when on the 3100-mile track).

Daughter Alakananda helping me at the race

In the 3100-mile race, we must be careful with our diet from the first thing in the morning until the end of the day. Once Sri Chinmoy told Suprabha, the first woman to run the 3100-mile race, that she had to eat after each

Holistic nutrition for the ultra-marathon runner

lap, even if she didn't want to. Otherwise, he said, she wouldn't last 20 minutes. Our body does have its rules, which must be obeyed. During the multi-day race, if your body shows uneven ups-and-downs, most likely it has to do with an inadequate dietary regime.

Another good helper of mine at morn - Satyagraha

Personally, I usually ask my helpers to split my breakfast, consisting of an omelet, mashed potatoes, and a salad, for instance, into small portions for me to take as I slow down for a short bite. I repeat on the next lap, and then the next, so it can take hours for me to eat my whole breakfast.

What is good about this approach is that it does not shock my stomach with great amounts of food all at once, and allows me to prolong the energy output obtained from food. The last lap at 23:30 is the only exception to this practice. The track is closed from midnight to 6 am, while we are having a rest in rented apartments. I walk this lap, to tell my body that that's all for the day, and I eat a normal meal right at the track, so that I won't have to think about it at home, as well as to ensure a good start the next morning.

Just like everybody else, I suffer from a technological tendency these days, when natural goods are so often replaced by those processed with synthetic additives, which make the products cheaper but not at all healthful. In the U.S., most juice brands contain synthetic vitamin C. My body rebels against it during the race in particular, giving me heartburn or even a rash all over my legs and feet. During training, when I have time restrictions due to my busy every-day schedule, I had to drink apple juice or other juices from the local supermarkets. I always paid the price for all of those synthetic additives, for example, flavorings, preservatives, sugar syrup, and so on. During the first week of a race I felt completely poisoned. For all those years I knew the truth. I realized what damaged me, as I compared my reactions to supermarket juice and fresh homemade juice, made with our own vegetables and fruits, grown with love and care. It wasn't until 2010 that I refused to have any store-bought drinks, no matter how much the tempo of modern life made it easy to take them. Still, we need a certain amount of time to cover the distance between knowledge and action.

Kinesiological Muscle Testing

When I came to my first 3100-mile race in the summer of 2004, I had no idea about correct eating on the track, although my previous running experience told me I needed vitamins as well as a good diet. Some 6- and 10-day runners recommended particular brands, which I managed to find, and also recommended that I take multivitamins, like calcium, magnesium etc. So, I brought Duovit vitamins, which I had taken during my training back in Kiev. That's when the troubles started! After several days of taking Duovit I felt no effect at all, while my body underwent the punishing schedule described above. What's more, I had some kind of a rash on my legs during the first few weeks, and I felt somewhat poisoned. As I was told later, it was the detoxification process my body was undergoing to eliminate the preservatives, additives etc., which got dumped there after our 'perfect' eating habits along with food industry marvels.

I would like to say a few words about the medical staff on the 3100-mile track. These volunteers, including the chiropractors, are well-educated and highly experienced. It's not a traditional medicine approach, to be able to find a problem by observing the patient's bodily reactions and to prescribe the particular medicine exactly suitable for each runner, in just 10-15 minutes. It was those experts who told me that each medicine should be tested to make sure that it exactly matches your system.

I have a story for you. By the time of my second race, I had become more experienced, and I had a whole list of vitamins and supplements that were necessary for me. Iron supplementation, for example, is highly useful under the increased exertion level during the first days of the body's adjustment to the 3100-mile race. In the U.S., a supplement called 'Ferrofood' is available. Since I could not find the specific brand prescribed for me at my previous race, I bought another one, thinking that it must be the same ferrum, after all! After three or four days on the track, I became unable to run at all. I felt some kind of energy blockage and energy loss in my feet. Our chiropractor, Pradhan from Chicago, asked me questions about my diet and the supplements I used. When it came to what kind of ferrum I was taking, Pradhan asked me to show him the package, which I did. That brand turned out to be unsuitable for me, and that's what blocked my energy. I was shocked and astonished at the news. Since that time, it became a strict rule for me to test even the most popular vitamin and supplement brands for personal suitability. So, when someone offers me something new to try, saying it's the best for recovery, it's the vitamins a certain team uses on a regular basis etc., I always respond, that I need to see and test that particular product on myself before I decide whether I will use it or not.

Now, let's talk about the test itself. It turns out that our body instantly and definitely shows its reaction to everything we offer it. What we need to do is just to learn its language, which is easier than you may think. It's our own

Holistic nutrition for the ultra-marathon runner

body, after all. Who can know it better than we do? However, sometimes our mind needs an interpreter. This role often goes to the doctors we turn to. You can consider yourself lucky if you consult a good doctor, not one who was a C student in school. There are plenty of those, I'm afraid...

Indeed, we were lucky to have really qualified doctors at the race. I trusted most of them, which is also important. Granted, I might have not fully understood their actions and prescriptions, but I did trust them. That's how it was with the kinesiological testing I am about to describe. The essence of the test is to compare the reaction of our body in the presence or absence of a certain medicine. The trick is that one doesn't have to really take this medicine internally. The simplified version of the test is as follows: you stand with your right hand extended alongside the body, palm faced outwards; you lift that arm on the right side to 90 degrees. The assistant, who's helping you test your body, tries to push the arm down, while you resist as much as you can; this is how you define the base reference point. Then, you hold the medicine in question with your left hand, and with your left hand holding the medicine at the center of your chest, you repeat the pushing test with your right arm. If you see that your capacity to resist does not decrease, and even increases, then this medicine suits you. It is sure to help you and give more strength to your body. Should the resistance decrease, you can be sure that this product won't do you any good.

What I have described here are just the basics of this approach. Chiropractors know many acupoints to press, and then are able to observe the reaction of the limbs, which clearly highlights the weaknesses of our body, from joint or bone displacement to general weakness of body functions. Once I felt such muscle tension at the upper back of my leg, that I couldn't push off properly when running. I went to a doctor. It took him only five minutes to determine that the problem was not in my leg at all, but that it was rather a nerve entrapment in my spine. Ten minutes later, the problem was solved. What a marvel!

It's worth adding, that if a person has previous experience with muscle testing, and is receptive to the method, one can carry out this test on himself without any assistance, by using the strength of one's right fist and holding the medicine in the left. This test is a wonderful thing, actually, able to sort out not only physical but also mental issues. We can determine in this way even the music that we need most in this or that situation. Our body is a skillful story teller, which we must learn to listen to!

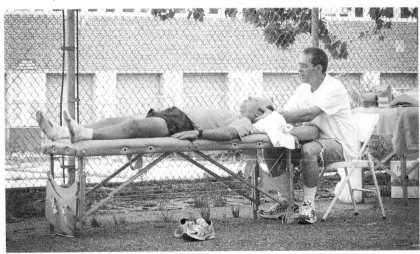

Dr. Pradhan is determining with the help of the kinesiological test what's wrong with my neck

Alkaline Balance

Doing my ultra-races, I learned that the body functions best when it is maintained in an alkaline condition. Great and prolonged exertions increase acidity in the body, so when we run ultra-races we need to help our body to get back to balance. The disturbed balance can manifest as general fatigue, apathy, or heartburn after drinking apple juice. During the years when I was running the 3,100-mile race, I learned how to deal with the problem. I eliminated any acidic products (apple juice, pineapple, vinegar etc.) in the afternoon. There are special pills to treat heartburn (I will discuss them later). I also discovered the beneficial effect of coral calcium water, which I drink after 2 pm during the race. Foods and supplements vary in their alkalinity. To ensure sustained efficiency, one must use them carefully, especially when feeling tired. Below is a list of the alkalinity and acidity levels of a variety of popular foods:

High alkalinity products: vegetables, fresh fruit, most fresh juices, potatoes and lettuce;

Low alkalinity products: dried fruit, unpasteurized milk and mushrooms.

Low acidity products: farmer cheese, nuts and unrefined flour products;

High acidity products: meat, sausage, fish, eggs, cheese, sweets, most starchy foods, alcohol and coffee.

Using many high acidity products on a regular basis may lead to super-acidulation in our body.

There is an amazing thing many scientists have acknowledged: positive emotions like joy and laughter increase alkalinity in our body, leaving the high alkalinity products behind! Each of us has experienced the situation when, after a funny joke or a friend's warm support, our fatigue vanished as if by magic. This is one of the reasons I like the Self-Transcendence 3100-mile race. All the participants realize that to finish the race they must compete with themselves, and also support others. Never have I seen more sincere, selfless and worthy people than those participating in the 3100-mile race. This has made me join them at the starting line over and over again. I love the atmosphere of oneness and sincerity, when everything is 100% genuine and real!

Here is one of Sri Chinmoy's aphorisms, which unveils the secret of how to deal with running ultra-races:

Remain cheerful,
For nothing destructive can pierce through
The adamantine wall of cheerfulness.
[Ten Thousand Flower-Flames, Part 39, #3891, New York, Agni Press, 1982]

By remaining happy, without whining or blaming others, you are able to balance your digestion, and even avoid some serious injuries, like problems with the achil-

Holistic nutrition for the ultra-marathon runner

les heel and sore muscles. This is a kind of art and courage that can be learned and developed. For more information, you can read Sri Chinmoy's books on sports, or any of my previous books (see the references at the end of this book).

Also there are "antioxidants," which remove free radicals, and support the alkaline balance of our body. They are even believed to slow down the aging process. Antioxidants are contained mostly in fresh fruit and in products they are added to (juices, iced tea, fruit puree etc.). The following fruits are particularly rich in antioxidants: bilberry, grapes, cranberries, ashberry, currants, and pomegranates. Green tea is one of the richest sources among the drinks.

There is a range of natural and synthetic medicines with high amounts of antioxidants, aimed at maintaining the necessary alkaline level, thus reducing fatigue, and improving one's performance and recovery. Again, it was during the 3100-mile race that I learned that antioxidant supplements were intentionally used by some runners during ultra-marathons. In the last few years of my running practice, I've been using Microhydrine, which has turned to be highly useful. I take several pills after 6 pm, and enjoy the sense of calm floating till midnight, and then I take them again for general recovery before going to bed.

In the next chapter I will present an article describing some of the newest research on ionized water, by my good friend and frequent helper at the 3100-mile race, Dr. Kausal Cortella of Italy. This article describes what could become another revolution in maintaining an alkaline balance in the body.

Ionized Water

by Dr. Kausal C. Cortella, Ph.D; N.D.; Race Medical Staff; www.solsociety.ch

I believe that quality water can be of tremendous assistance to runners, especially to the amazing efforts of ultra-long distance runners like the 3100-mile race runners.

Not all waters are equally good, nor are they all equally effective! On the contrary many problems can come from water.

After almost 15 years as a researcher in the field of water, and after having published books and articles all over the world, I came to the conclusion that the 3100-mile runners should drink only ionized-energized water during the race.

What is ionized-energized water?

All life on earth is thought to have arisen from water. The bodies of all living organisms are composed largely of water. About 70 to 90 percent of all organic matter is water. The chemical reactions in all plants and animals that support life take place in a water medium. Water not only provides the medium to make these life-sustaining reactions possible, but water itself is often an important reactant or product of these reactions.

To understand the function of water in maintaining energy and strength, we need to understand the meaning of reduction, oxidation and redox potential (ORP). Reduction means the addition of an electron (e-), and its converse, oxidation means the removal of an electron. The addition of an electron, reduction, stores energy in the reduced compound. The removal of an electron, oxidation, liberates energy from the oxidized compound. Whenever one substance is reduced, another is oxidized. In biological systems, removal or addition of an electron constitutes the most frequent mechanism of oxidation-reduction reactions. These oxidation-reduction reactions are frequently called redox reactions.

An acid is a substance that increases the concentration of hydrogen ions (H+) in water. A base is a substance that decreases the concentration of hydrogen ions, in other words, increasing the concentration of hydroxide ions OH-. The degree of acidity or alkalinity of a solution is measured in terms of a value known as pH, which is the negative logarithm of the concentration of hydrogen ions.

At pH 7, water contains equal concentrations of H+ and OH- ions. Substances with a pH higher than 7 are alkaline because they contain a higher concentration of OH- than H+.

Importance of balancing pH

Most of the free radicals (active oxygen is one of the worst of them) with unpaired electrons are unstable and have a high oxidation potential, which means they are capable of stealing electrons from other cells, healthy cells. This chemical mechanism is very useful in disinfectants such as hydrogen peroxide and ozone which can be used to sterilize wounds or medical instruments.

Problems arise, however, when too many of these active oxygen molecules, or free radicals, are produced in the body, such as during a race not to speak about a long distance race. They are extremely reactive and can also attach themselves to normal, healthy cells and damage them genetically. These active oxygen radicals steal electrons from normal, healthy biological molecules. This electron theft by active oxygen oxidizes tissue and can cause disease and pain.

Because active oxygen can damage normal tissue, it is essential to scavenge this active oxygen from the body before it can cause disintegration of healthy tissue.

The solution is water but not all waters are equal! If we can find an effective method to block the oxidation of healthy tissue by active oxygen, then we can attempt to prevent disease and injuries.

One way to protect healthy tissue from the ravages of oxidation caused by active oxygen is to provide free electrons to active oxygen radicals, thus neutralizing their high oxidation potential and preventing them from reacting with healthy tissue.

In natural medicine, we believe that substances that prevent oxidation - called ANTIOXIDANTS - can block the damage (e.g., vitamin C, vitamin E, beta-carotene, selenium). Indeed these substances are infinitely less effective than ionized-energized water!

Water, the natural solution

Water treated by electrolysis to increase its reduction potential is the best solution to the problem of providing a safe source of free electrons to block the oxidation of normal tissue by free oxygen radicals. I believe that reduced water, water with an excess of free electrons to donate to active oxygen, is the best solution because:

The reduction potential of water can be dramatically greater than the antioxidants in food or vitamin supplements.

The molecule weight of reduced water is low, making it fast-acting and able to reach all tissues of the body in a very short time.

What is IONIZED WATER?

Ionized water is the product of mild electrolysis which takes place in the ionized water unit. Ionized water is treated tap water that has not only been filtered, but has also been reformed so that it provides reduced water with a large mass of electrons that can be donated to active oxygen in the body to block the oxidation of normal cells.

Redox potential, not pH, is the crucial factor here.

Traditionally we have judged the properties of water from the standpoint of pH, in other words, whether water is acidic or alkaline.

The importance of pH has been over-emphasized. But, unfortunately, nothing has been discussed about ORP, or oxidation-reduction potential.

The pH of tap water is about pH 7, or neutral. When

tap water is electrolyzed into Ionized Water, its reduced water has a pH of about 9. Even if you make alkaline water of pH 9 by adding sodium hydroxide or make acidic water of pH 3 by adding hydrogen chloride, you will find very little change in the ORP values of the two waters. On the other hand, when you divide tap water with electrolysis, you can see the ORP fluctuate by as much as +- 1,000 mV. By electrolysis we can obtain reduced water with negative potential that is good for the body.

When taken internally, the reduced Ionized Water with its redox potential of -250 to -350 mV readily donates its electrons to oddball oxygen radicals and blocks the interaction of the active oxygen with normal molecules.

When taken internally, the effects of reduced water are immediate. Ionized Water inhibits excessive fermentation in the digestive tract by indirectly reducing metabolites such as hydrogen sulfide, ammonia, histamines, indoles, phenols and scatoles, resulting in better digestion and liver detox.

In 1965, the Ministry of Welfare of Japan announced that reduced water obtained from electrolysis can prevent abnormal fermentation of intestinal microbes.

Ionized Water superior to antioxidant diet

Today we read much about correct dieting principles and paying attention to what we eat in order to stay healthy. This is a sensible practice, but it is surprising that many of us don't realize that the bulk of what we eat is composed of water. Vegetables and fruits are 90% water; fish and meat are about 70% water as well.

Ionized Water, with its low molecular weight and high

reduction potential, makes it a superior scavenging agent of active oxygen. But electrolysis inside the Ionized Water unit not only charges the reduced water with electrons, it also reduces the size of reduced water molecule clusters.

The clusterization of water is a process similar to energization of water. You can see three pictures of the same water after having been ionized and also energized with Ojas Krug.

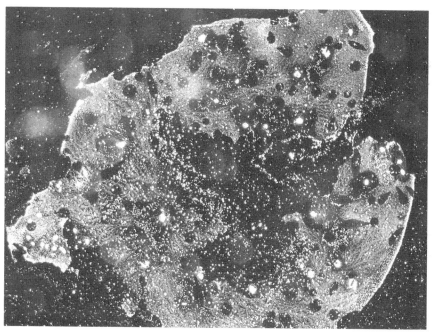

Untreated tap water

Eat to Run

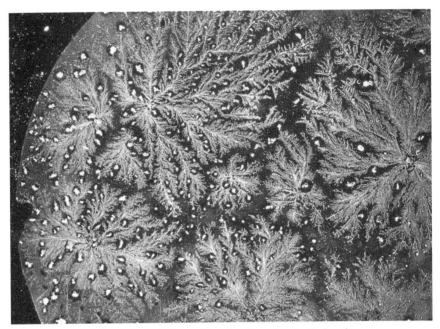

Tap water filtered ionized and alkalinized

Tap water filtered ionized, alkalinized and Ojas energized

The ordered clusterized water is more readily absorbed by the body than untreated tap water. Ionized Water quickly permeates the body and blocks the oxidation of biological molecules by donating its abundant electrons to active oxygen, enabling biological molecules to replace themselves naturally without the damage caused by the oxidation that can cause diseases.

Downstream from the digestive tract, starting at the liver, reduced water quickly enters the liver and other organs due to, first, its lower molecular weight, and, second, the size of its clusters. At tissue sites throughout the body, reduced water with its safe, yet potent reduction potential readily donates its passenger electrons freely to active oxygen and neutralizes them so they cannot damage the molecules of healthy cells. Normal cells are protected from the electron thievery of active oxygen and allowed to grow, mature, function and regenerate without interference from rogue, oddball oxygen radicals, which tend to steal the electrons from the molecules of normal, healthy biological molecules.

I fully believe that during the race all of the runners should drink this special water, avoiding the use of simply filtered water or bottled mineral water, which are both strongly acidic for the body!

~~~

In 2014 for the first time I was using ionized water during trainings and the race itself. It surpassed my expectations!

What I can say for sure - this kind of water helps you to

Eat to Run

recover much faster. Even during my 15 minutes breakes during the day at 3100 Mile Race recovery progress was quite visible. Not to say about our long night breakes - almost all mornings at our regular 6 am start my legs were «brand new».

Here is some statistics what I achieved for the first time during the race in 2014:

- 6 days out of 48 I did more than 70 miles
- last 3 days prior to the finish day - 70, 70 and 71 miles
- last day - super pace: 20 miles in 3 hours 57 minutes. Under the rain with heavy shoes
- best miles during the race - 130 laps, 71 miles - day number 48
- first 10 days - 644 miles, second 10 days - 633 miles, third 10 days - 614 miles, forth 10 days - 649 miles, last full 10 days - 674 miles.
- first 1550 miles of the race - 24 days + 12:55:36, second 1550 miles - 23 days +15:01:43
- average speed - 64.366 miles per day (103,587 km)
- day of full moon (which was always the weakest) - 60 miles
- weight loss by 7 kg. First and last 10 days my weight did not change
- fast recovery. Already after one week after finish I started training for 6-8 km per day and in 3 week time ran 47 mile race in a time of 7:20:30. (pace - 9:14 per mile or 5:44 per 1 km)

During 3100 Mile Race I was using Chanson Miracle MAX Water Ionizer with C3 Pre-filter. You could learn more about it following the link **www.bitly.com/miracleMAX**

Fats And Their Breakdown

As I have mentioned already, fats make up the main source of fuel during a multi-day race. Most of our energy comes from their breakdown. However, after about 20 days of one race, I noticed some fluctuations in my strength, which turned out to depend on two things. The first is a fat deficiency. This can be compensated for by products containing vegetable oils: avocado, cashew, olive oil etc. The second reason is that after three weeks of running, even with proper nutrition, fats start to break down reluctantly. This phenomenon is rather widespread. So, I have decided to talk about this as well.

Fats are known to break down with the help of biliary acid. Gall ducts transport bile from the liver and the gall bladder to the intestines. The polluted gall ducts may cause fat breakdown problems, preventing bile transportation. No runners tried to treat this problem during the race due to possible risks of treatment. Nevertheless, there are certain medicines we have used to clean the liver and gall ducts several weeks before the race, as a preventive measure. To clean the liver often means to clean the gall ducts.

Often vegetarians have problems digesting greasy food, which makes them overweight sometimes. This factor is critical during the multi-day races. We've found two possible solutions to this. First is a well-known fat-burning amino acid called L-carnitine. Body builders use it to get rid of extra-weight, while it helps ordinary people to add energy to the muscles. I would like to note, though, that this works only under an intense workload.

The second solution is represented by Medium-Chain Triglycerides oil, widely known simply as MCT oil, based on coconut oil. Due to its special qualities, our body processes it as easily as carbohydrates, and with the same energy effect as fats give.

We found a great relief with that MCT oil, especially if extreme load takes longer than 20 days. In any case, MCT oil is belonging to a healthy vegetarian diet.

Vitamins And Supplements

My long-term experience on this topic is reflected in the table below. It contains vitamins and supplements that help me cope with an extreme energy load over the course of 50 days or so. Please, remember that despite the availability of the general strategy, the particular brands, details and regime issues must be approached individually. You could use a kinesiological test, as described above, for example. However, there are other ways known to experts in alternative medicine,

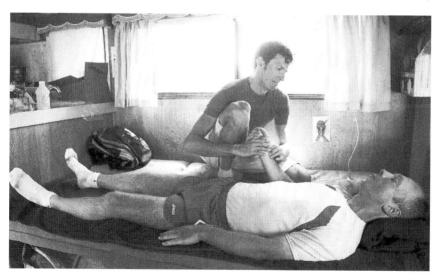

Dr. Kausal is checking me by pulse in the race minivan

which help specify not only the suitability of a particular medical product, but also a regimen for using it. I have experienced myself the ability of Kausal, an outstanding naturopathic and Ayurvedic doctor, to make a quick and super-precise diagnosis, choose a proper medicine, and develop a regimen only by taking my pulse.

Complete table is for 3100-mile race. The last column contains my recommendations for a 6- or 10-day race.

Name	Brand	Comments	6/10
(C) Vitamin C **1000 mg** Non-acidic Vitamin C Supplements. Vegetarian	Country Life	Immune system reinforcement, antioxidant. Four times a day	*
(L) L-lysine 500mg. vegetable capsules	Solgar, Country Life	Amino acid for immune system reinforcement; A must when having cold or suffering from fatigue! 2-3 times a day	*
(P) Pantothenic acid 500mg. suitable for vegetarians	Solgar	Immune system reinforcement. 2-3 times a day	
(B) Complete B-complex	Amway	Muscle recovery. Every 4-6 hours	*
(AF) A-F beta-food	Standard Process	Essential under intense performance of quadriceps and other muscles of thigh. 1-2 times a day	*

Holistic nutrition for the ultra-marathon runner

(T) Trace minerals (liquid form)	Luqui mins	Mineral complex of marine origin. 1-2 times a day	
CALM Calcium-magnesium	Peter Gillham	Bones, excitatory system, alkaline balance 2 times a day	*
Alca-Mine Soluble calcium	Coral club	Take as potion. Renovates alkaline balance, particularly afternoons	*
(FE) Ferrofood	Standard Process	Hematonic. Critical during first few days of a race. For thigh flexors - 'iron' muscles. 2 times a day	*
(MU) Multi-vitamins «Multi 100»	Country Life	General vitamin balance. 2 times a day	*
L-carnitine	Now sports	Amino-acid for fats disintegration (fatburning), 1-2 times a day	
(Mi) Microhydrine	Coral Club	Strong antioxidant. Taken in the evening it gave a nice floating sensation for the rest of the day. Taken right before bedtime, it served for recovery. Can't be combined with taking ferrum.	*
Tums	USA	For alkaline balance. Pills for heartburn. Several pills for each case	*

MCT oil	Now sports	Miracle fat, digested as carbohydrates. Based on coconut oil. One table spoon, with meal only	
(VEGA) Performance Protein	Vega Sport	Muscles recovery and building up. Right before bedtime. Not to be confused with protein muscle nutrition for better performance under exertions.	*

Regimen:

6:00	C
10:00	B, L
12:00	FE, CALM, MU
14:00	C, P, B
16:00	T, AF
18:00	C, MU, L, FE, CALM, B
20:00	Mi, T
23:00	C, B, VEGA, P, Mi

Since my aim was to display the supplements it is desirable to take during a multi-day race, the above table doesn't contain homeopathy, creams, gels and other external preparations for muscles, joints and ligaments, designed to keep the body and feet in perfect condition. There are plenty of those.

The Secret Ingredient

Everything I wrote about here definitely works. However, as I described above, the alkaline balance is extremely dependent on our inner state. The 3100-mile race is obviously a very extreme and long one. Many factors must come together in order for a runner to overcome the challenge of this incredibly long distance: physical fitness, inner balance, proper diet, financial state, to name a few of the most important ones. I must say that proper alignment of those factors works only in the presence of one additional secret ingredient: belief in oneself.

I witnessed how even well-prepared runners had to drop out of the race, how a runner's desire for an ordinary daily life blocked his performance, how an excessively competitive spirit led to suffering and even injuries. This is a very special race. Nevertheless, the good news is that it's POSSIBLE to cover the distance! Many people who believe they could never run such a race are actually capable of doing it. We just need to know which strings to pull. One needs time, as well. Strange as it may seem, our body has enough flexibility to adjust to a new diet and work-load. More problems are created by our mind, which doubts and puts aside anything it can't explain, and is inclined to put things off.

The most time-consuming thing is to wake up and expand our consciousness. This is the reason why the 3100-mile race requires many years of preparation before our being is completely prepared for it. Some things just can't be omitted, and they shouldn't be. For more than 21 years I've been doing my meditation practice on Sri Chinmoy's path, and I have finished the 3100-mile race seven times now out of nine starts, but it was only after three years of participation in the 3100 that I was able to feel what "flying" means: nothing hurts, muscles recover themselves, you live a full life and you are above the Nature. That's because you are a Man with a role, given by the Supreme. I am lucky and happy to have found it!

I would like to tell you a story, which I told in one of my earlier books, *Believe in Yourself*, and which is iconic to me.

2006 race story

My self-belief training started the day I was SET to fly to New York. My wife, my daughter and I arrived at the Boryspil airport 50 minutes before the departure time, only to discover that we had left our passports at home! My wife and my daughter went white at the news. It was clearly impossible to go home, pick up the passports and return on time. Despite this fact, I decided to try. That's when the adventures began.

Instead of the usual 40 minutes one-way, the taxi driver

made the round trip in 40 minutes. On the way, I didn't allow myself to doubt our success - not even for a second. I was conscious that if I allowed that thought-thief to enter my mind, "That's it - we are late, we will need to change our tickets, etc." - we would not have a flight that day. My tremendous peace and confidence were my saviours.

The next time around, we entered the airport five minutes before the plane was scheduled to depart. The check-in manager turned out to be a good person and showed sympathy to me as the only Ukrainian runner in the world's longest race. She agreed to register us, but the computers refused to cooperate, because the check-in process had ended by that time. Despite her willingness, she could do nothing. I continued to insist, saying that possibly she could do it manually; it should be the machines that serve us, not vice versa. It was not until she called the plane and the pilot agreed to wait for us, that we were admitted onto the plane. When we finally took our seats, I managed to utter only: "I simply can't believe it! We've delayed the flight of an American 'Delta' for half an hour!"

That experience came to my mind quite often later in the race. The journey to your goal starts when you gain confidence in achieving it. No matter how many times you have finished the 3100-mile race, every time the distance challenges you anew. This faith differs from our impermanent presumptuousness or those vague I-can-do-it words. It grows, slowly but steadily, just like a seed inside you.

In 2006, I faced a great deal of hardship: heavy rains – the average rainfall for the month came down all in one single day; the necessity to run half-bent to overcome strong winds, which crushed trees in the neighborhood; forty degree centigrade heat, when other people in New York City were strictly advised to stay indoors; exhaustion and sleep hanging on my eyelids at 11 pm, etc. Each time I resorted to another of Sri Chinmoy's aphorisms, one that sends a thrill through my entire body:

*If we really want to go onward,
And fly upward and dive inward -
There is nothing
That can actually resist us.*

[CD: Journey Beyond Within]

Sri Chinmoy presenting me a trophy the next day after my first finish in the 3100-Mile Race. August 6, 2004

Recommended Books For Further Reading

Books by Sri Chinmoy

The Inner Running and the Outer Running, New York, Aum Publications, 2008

Down the sweep of centuries there have been many who, through God-given talent and discipline, became great runners. There have also been many who, through God-given capacity and inner discipline, became great spiritual figures, runners in the inner world.

A champion sprinter and decathlete in his youth, Sri Chinmoy took up long- distance running in his late forties, and in the span of seven years completed twenty-two marathons, three ultra-marathons, and countless shorter races. More important, his inner life of the spirit laid the philosophical foundation for the world's most respected ultra-distance running organisation, the Sri Chinmoy Marathon Team.

Sport and Meditation: The Inner Dimension of Sport, Nurnberg:The Golden Shore, 2012.

In this remarkable book, Sri Chinmoy reveals the inner aspect of sport —a dimension that everyone can add to his or her current physical and mental training.

It is this new dimension that enables us to enhance our physical performance, but also makes our satisfaction from sport deep and lasting.

Yoga and the Spiritual Life, New York: Aum Publications, 1996.

In this book Sri Chinmoy explains the philosophy of Yoga and Eastern mysticism. Written in a practical vein, it offers the newcomer as well as the advanced seeker a deep understanding of the spiritual life.

Of particular interest is the section devoted to questions and answers on the soul and the inner life. As an illumined Yogi who experienced these realities firsthand, Sri Chinmoy's answers offer a clarity and authenticity rarely encountered.

The Wisdom of Sri Chinmoy, San Diego, California: The Blue Dove Press, 2000.

This distillation of Sri Chimnoy's thought provides a clear summary of many elements of the author's philosophy and teachings. The book has selections covering the entire "A-Z" of spirituality, 71 sections in all, beginning with 'aspiration' and ending with 'Yoga'.

Books by Stutisheel

My first Ironman. *From dream to finish - 2013*

Esoteric Project Management. *The development and application of inner power in management - 2014*

Run. Journey. Become. *The 3100-Mile footrace of a lifetime - 2016*

Book by Grahak Cunningham, the 3100-Mile Race winner in 2012

Running Beyond the Marathon: *insights into the longest footrace in the world*, Pure Refreshment Publishing, 2012

Books are available in paperback and kindle format at www.Amazon.com

Additional Information

www.3100.SriChinmoyRaces.org - official page of the 3100-Mile Race

www.3100.Lebedev.org.ua – 3100-Mile Race blog

www.Stutisheel.org – official site of Stutisheel

www.SriChinmoy.org – official site of Sri Chinmoy

Made in the USA
Lexington, KY
14 March 2018